CONTENTS

ISBN 0-8497-6253-7

Unit 1
Note Values

Quarter Note   ← Stem   ← Note Head

A stem may go up or down on a note.
Up stems go on the **right** side of the note head.
Down stems go on the **left** side of the note head.

Up Stem   Down Stem

1. Draw up stems on these note heads.

2. Draw down stems on these note heads.

3. Draw four quarter notes with up stems.

4. Draw four quarter notes with down stems.

Half Note

One half note equals two quarter notes.

5. Draw four half notes with up stems.

6. Draw four half notes with down stems.

Dotted Half Note

One dotted half note equals three quarter notes.

The dot on the right side of the note head adds half of the value of the note.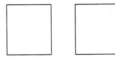

7. Draw four dotted half notes with up stems.

8. Draw four dotted half notes with down stems.

Whole Note o

One whole note equals four quarter notes.

9. The whole note has no stem. Draw four whole notes.

10. Write the names of these notes.

quarter   _____   _____   _____   _____

11. Answer these questions by drawing the correct note.

Eighth Notes

One Eighth Note

One eighth note has a flag on the stem.

12. Draw flags on these stems to form eighth notes.

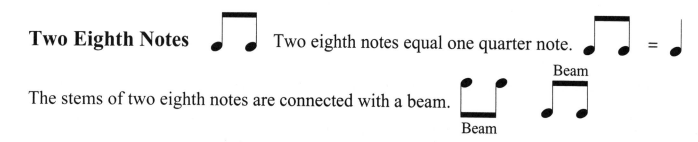

Two Eighth Notes

The stems of two eighth notes are connected with a beam.

13. Draw beams to connect these pairs of notes to form two eighth notes.

Four Eighth Notes

The stems of four eighth notes are connected with a beam.

14. Draw beams on these groups of notes to form four eighth notes.

Dotted Quarter Note

One dotted quarter note equals three eighth notes.

The dot on the right side of the note head adds
half of the value of the note.

15. Draw four dotted quarter notes, two with up stems and two with down stems.

Note Value Review

16. Write the names of these notes.

_____   _____   _____

_____   _____   _____

17. Answer these questions by drawing the correct note.

Unit 2
The Staff

Lines and Spaces

The staff has five lines and four spaces. The lines and spaces are numbered from the bottom to the top.

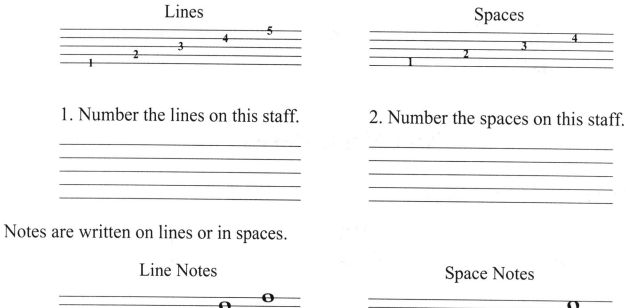

1. Number the lines on this staff.

2. Number the spaces on this staff.

Notes are written on lines or in spaces.

3. Write **L** for the line notes and **S** for the space notes.

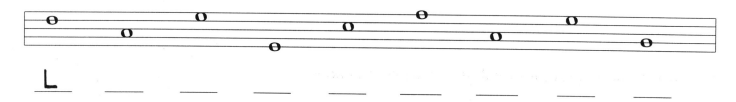

Notes **on or above** the third line have **down stems**.
Notes **below** the third line have **up stems**.

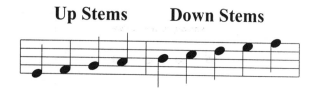

4. Draw stems on these note heads.

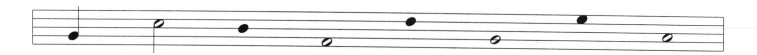

Clef Signs

A clef sign is used at the beginning of each staff.

Treble clef

Drawing Treble Clef Signs

5. Trace these steps for drawing treble clef signs, then draw your own.

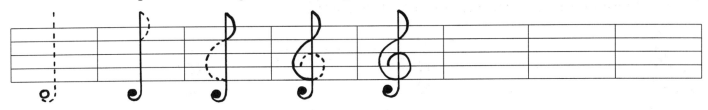

Bass clef

Drawing Bass Clef Signs

6. Trace these steps for drawing bass clef signs, then draw your own.

The Grand Staff

The **grand staff** is formed by joining the treble staff and bass staff with a **brace** and a **bar line**.

7. Trace these braces and bar lines to form grand staffs.

8. Draw braces and bar lines to form grand staffs.
   Draw treble and bass clef signs.

Bar Lines

Music on the staff is divided by **bar lines** into **measures.**
The end of a piece of music has a **double bar line.**

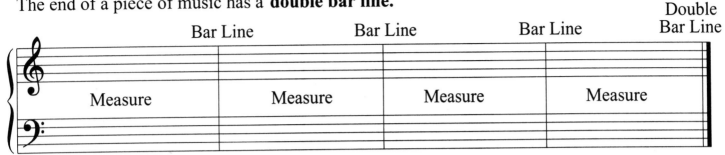

When dots are placed in front of a double bar line, it forms a **repeat sign.**
A repeat sign means to play the music again.

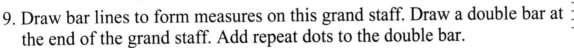

9. Draw bar lines to form measures on this grand staff. Draw a double bar at
   the end of the grand staff. Add repeat dots to the double bar.

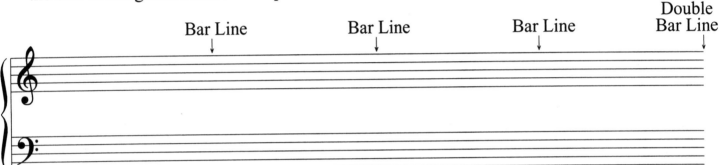

Review of the Staff

10. A staff has _____ lines and _____ spaces.

11. Notes are written on _____ or in _____ .

12. Notes written below the third line have _____ stems.

13. Notes written on or above the third line have _____ stems.

14. 𝄞 This is a _____ clef. 15. 𝄢 This is a _____ clef.

16. The grand staff is joined by a _____ and a _____ .

17. Bar lines divide music on the staff into _____ .

18. The end of a piece has a _____ .

19. :‖ This is a _____ sign.

Unit 3

Note Naming

Treble Clef Notes

Treble Clef Line Notes

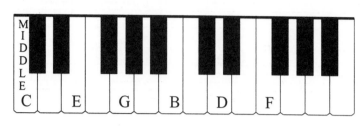

1. Name these treble clef line notes.

2. Draw these treble clef line notes. Use whole notes.

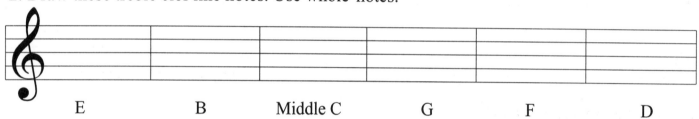

E   B   Middle C   G   F   D

Treble Clef Space Notes

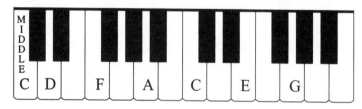

3. Name these treble clef space notes.

4. Draw these treble clef space notes. Use half notes.

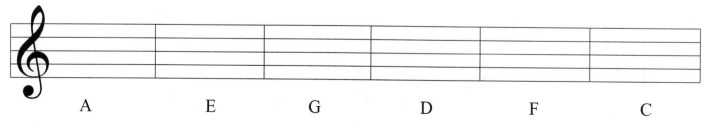

A   E   G   D   F   C

Bass Clef Notes

Bass Clef Line Notes

5. Name these bass clef line notes.

6. Draw these bass clef line notes. Use quarter notes.

G	Middle C	D	F	A	B

Bass Clef Space Notes

7. Name these bass clef space notes.

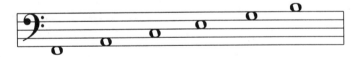

8. Draw these bass clef space notes. Use whole notes.

A	E	G	B	F	C

Naming Notes on the Grand Staff

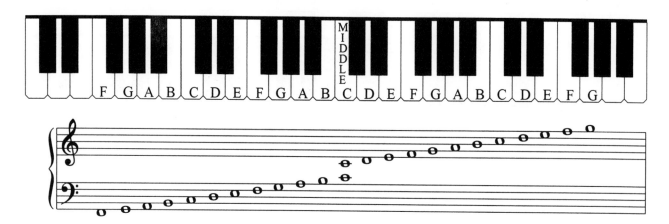

9. Name these notes on the grand staff.

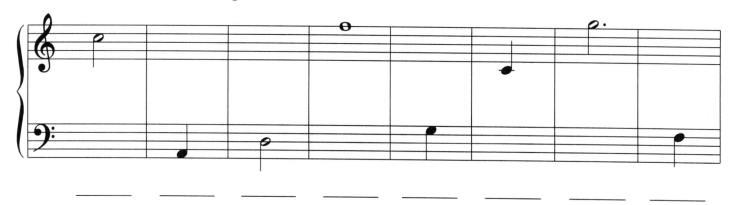

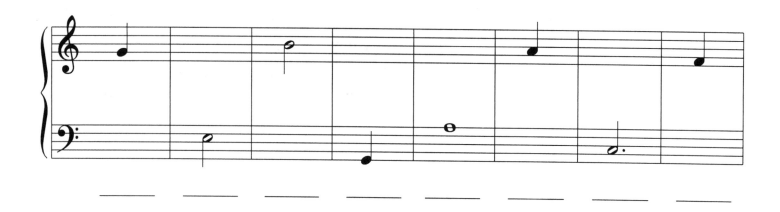

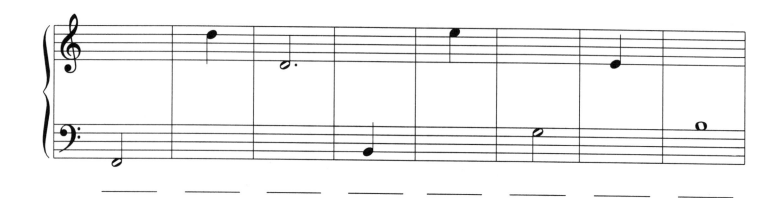

Drawing Notes on the Grand Staff

10. Draw these LINE notes on the grand staff. Use half notes.

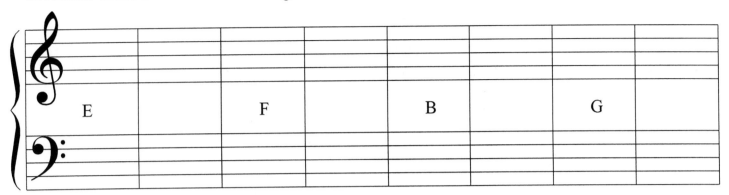

11. Draw these SPACE notes on the grand staff. Use whole notes.

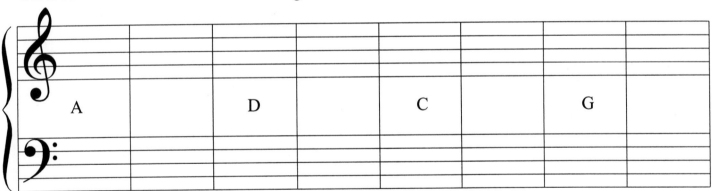

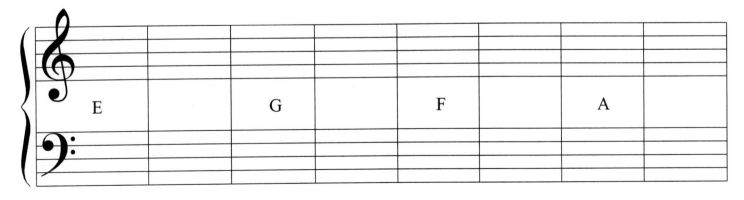

Unit 4
Time Signatures and Rhythm

The **time signature** is the two numbers written at the beginning of a piece.
- The top number tells how many beats are in each measure.
- The bottom number tells what kind of note gets one beat.

Time Signature ²₄

2 means two beats in each measure.
4 means the quarter note gets one beat.   ♩ = 1 beat

                                              ♩ = 2 beats

1. Clap and count this rhythm aloud.

Count: 1   2   1   2   *(continue counting)*

2. Write the counts under the notes. Clap and count aloud.

3. Add bar lines to this rhythm.
   Write the counts under the notes. Clap and count aloud.

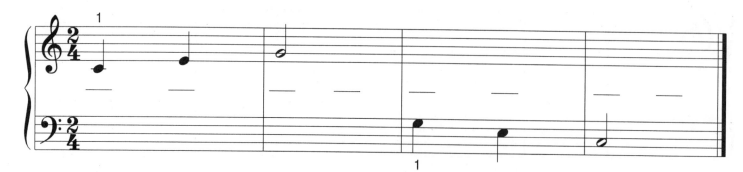

4. Write in the counts. Play and count aloud.

Time Signature ¾

3 means three beats in each measure.
4 means the quarter note gets one beat.

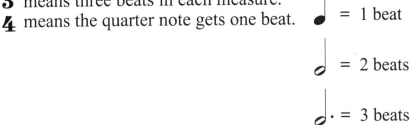

♩ = 1 beat

𝅗𝅥 = 2 beats

𝅗𝅥. = 3 beats

5. Clap and count this rhythm aloud.

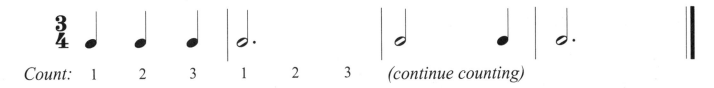

Count: 1   2   3   1   2   3   *(continue counting)*

6. Write the counts under the notes. Clap and count aloud.

7. Add bar lines to this rhythm.
   Write the counts under the notes. Clap and count aloud.

8. Write in the counts. Play and count aloud.

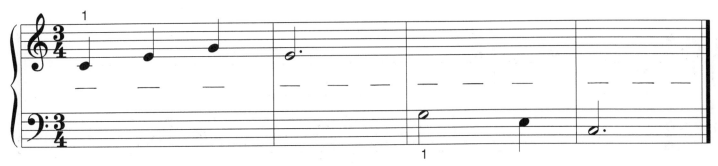

Time Signature 4/4

4 means four beats in each measure.
4 means the quarter note gets one beat.

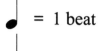

= 1 beat

= 2 beats

= 3 beats

o = 4 beats

9. Clap and count this rhythm aloud.

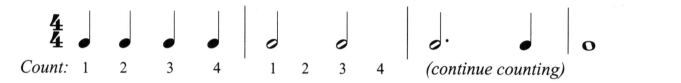

Count: 1 2 3 4 1 2 3 4 *(continue counting)*

10. Write the counts under the notes. Clap and count aloud.

11. Add bar lines to this rhythm.
Write the counts under the notes. Clap and count aloud.

12. Write in the counts. Play and count aloud.

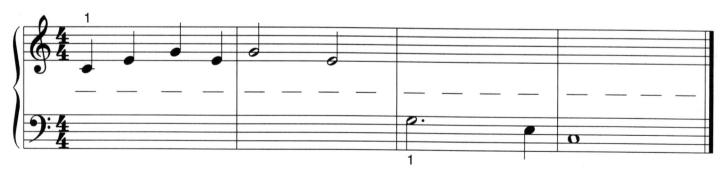

GP660

Counting Eighth Notes

Eighth notes may be counted by saying "and" after the number.

13. Clap and count this rhythm aloud.

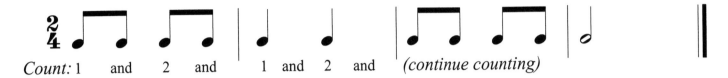

Count: 1   and   2   and   1   and   2   and   *(continue counting)*

14. Write the counts under the notes. Use a + sign for the word "and".
    Clap and count aloud.

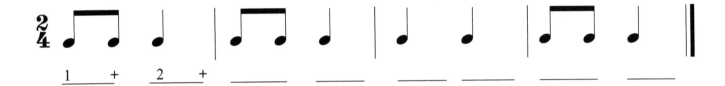

   1   +   2   +   ___ ___   ___ ___   ___ ___   ___ ___

15. Add bar lines to this rhythm.
    Write the counts under the notes. Clap and count aloud.

16. Write in the counts. Play and count aloud.

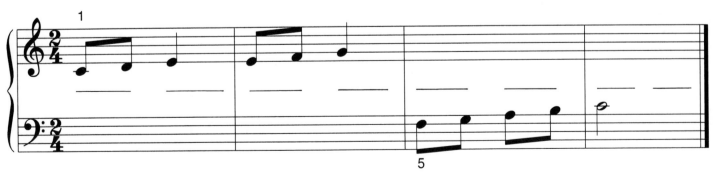

17. Clap and count this rhythm aloud.

Count: 1 and 2 and 3 and   *(continue counting)*

A group of four eighth notes
may be joined with one beam.

1   and   2   and   3   and   1 and 2   and   3   and

18. Write the counts under the notes. Use a + sign for the word "and".
    Clap and count aloud.

19. Add bar lines to this rhythm.
    Write the counts under the notes. Clap and count aloud.

20. Write in the counts. Play and count aloud.

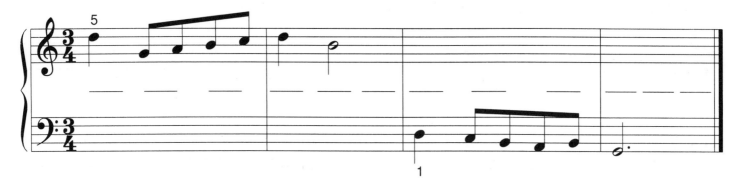

21. Clap and count this rhythm aloud.

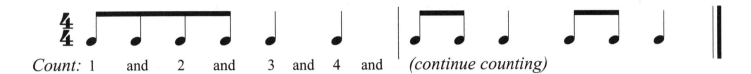

Count: 1   and   2   and   3   and   4   and   *(continue counting)*

22. Write the counts under the notes. Use a + sign for the word "and".
    Clap and count aloud.

23. Add a bar line to this rhythm.
    Write the counts under the notes. Clap and count aloud.

24. Write in the counts. Play and count aloud.

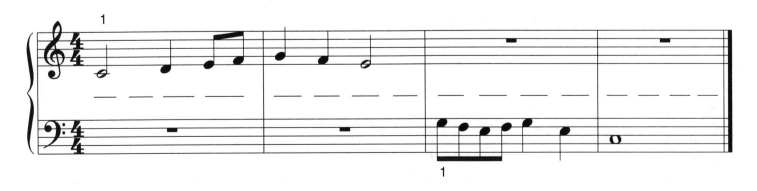

Counting Dotted Quarter Notes and Eighth Notes

The dotted quarter note is often followed by one eighth note.

A dotted quarter note and one eighth note equal two quarter notes.

or one half note.

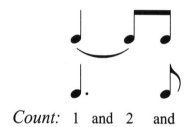

A dotted quarter note followed by one eighth note may be understood when seen as a tied note.

Count: 1 and 2 and

25. Write the counts under these notes. Clap and count aloud.
    Play and count aloud.

(Right Hand)

1 + 2 +

(Left Hand)

(Right Hand)

GP660

Upbeats

An **upbeat** is the note or notes that come before the first full measure of a piece.

The measure with the upbeat (s) is **incomplete.**
The missing counts are found in the last measure, which is also incomplete.

26. Clap and count these rhythms aloud.

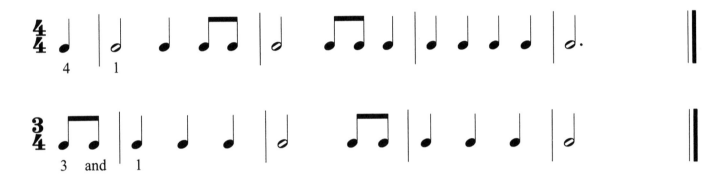

27. Play and count aloud.

Rest Signs

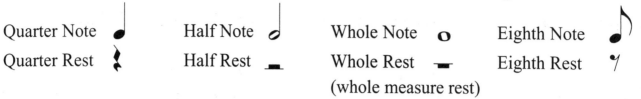

Rest signs are used in music for **silence**. These notes have rest signs of the same value.

Quarter Note   Half Note   Whole Note   Eighth Note

Quarter Rest   Half Rest   Whole Rest   Eighth Rest
(whole measure rest)

28. Draw each rest four times.

Quarter Rest   Half Rest

Whole Rest   Eighth Rest

29. Draw a rest to complete the correct number of beats in each measure.
Clap and count these rhythms aloud.

Matching and Crossword Puzzle

1. Draw a line to connect each sign with its term.

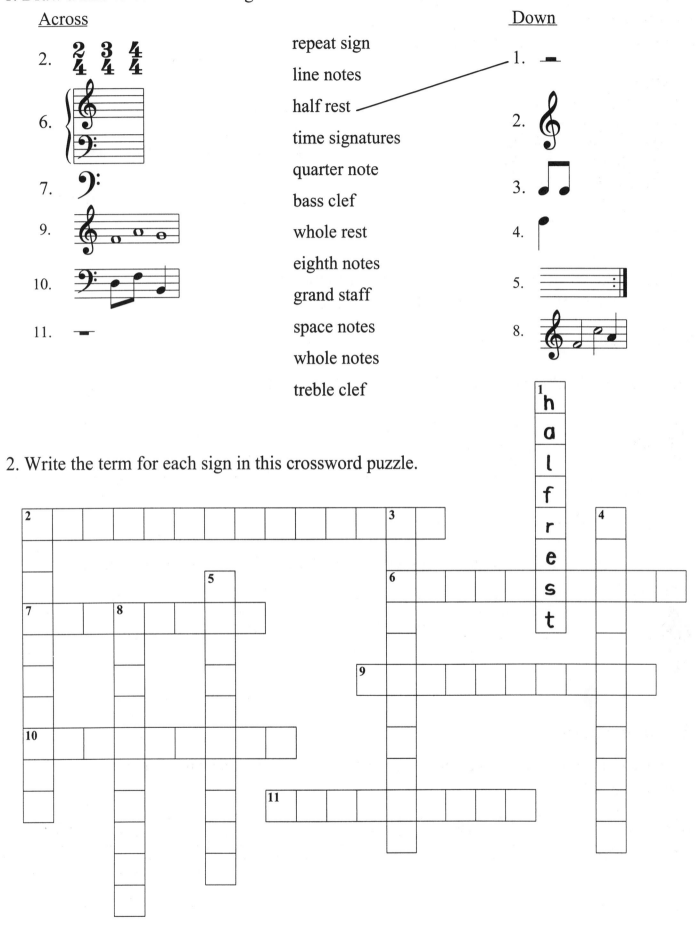

Across
2.
6.
7.
9.
10.
11.

repeat sign
line notes
half rest
time signatures
quarter note
bass clef
whole rest
eighth notes
grand staff
space notes
whole notes
treble clef

Down
1.
2.
3.
4.
5.
8.

2. Write the term for each sign in this crossword puzzle.

Unit 5
Intervals

An **interval** is the distance between two notes.
Melodic intervals are two notes played *one at a time.*
Harmonic intervals are two notes played *at the same time.*

2nds

2nds on the keyboard

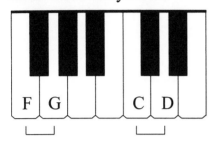

2nds on the staff

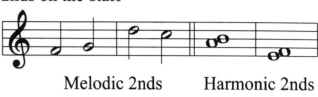

Melodic 2nds   Harmonic 2nds

2nds on the keyboard are from one white key to the very next white key.
2nds on the staff are from a line to the next space **or** a space to the next line.

Melodic 2nds

1. Draw a melodic 2nd **up** from each given note. Use quarter notes. Name each note.

2. Draw a melodic 2nd **down** from each given note. Use half notes. Name each note.

Harmonic 2nds

3. Draw a note **above** each given note to form harmonic 2nds. Use whole notes.
   Name the notes.

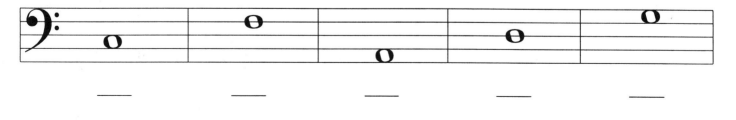

3rds

3rds on the keyboard

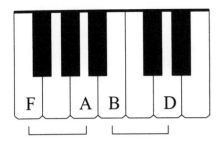

3rds on the staff

Melodic 3rds   Harmonic 3rds

3rds on the keyboard skip one white key.

3rds on the staff move from a space to the next space **or** a line to the next line.

Melodic 3rds

4. Draw a melodic 3rd **up** from each given note. Use quarter notes. Name each note.

5. Draw a melodic 3rd **down** from each given note. Use half notes. Name each note.

Harmonic 3rds

6. Draw a note above each given note to form harmonic 3rds. Use whole notes. Name the notes.

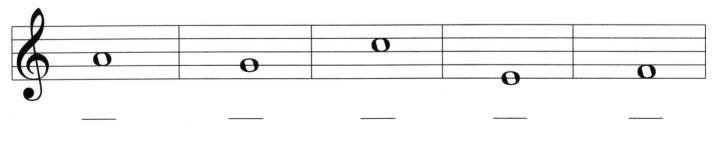

7. Name each interval (2nd or 3rd).

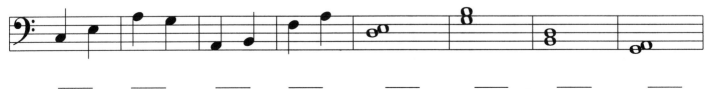

4ths

4ths on the keyboard

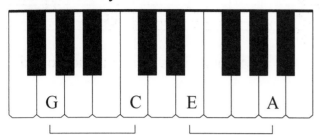

4ths on the staff

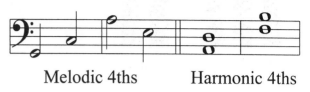

Melodic 4ths   Harmonic 4ths

4ths on the keyboard skip two white keys.
4ths on the staff move from a space to a line **or** a line to a space, skipping one space and one line

Melodic 4ths

8. Draw a melodic 4th **up** from each given note. Use quarter notes. Name each note.

9. Draw a melodic 4th **down** from each given note. Use half notes. Name each note.

Harmonic 4ths

10. Draw a note above each given note to form harmonic 4ths. Use whole notes. Name the notes.

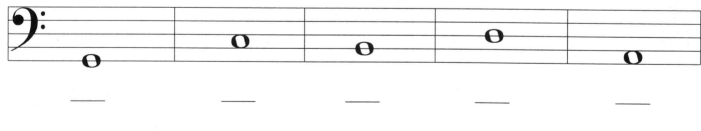

11. Name each interval (2nd, 3rd or 4th).

5ths

5ths on the keyboard

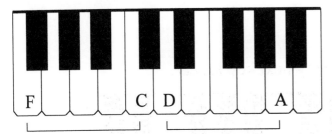

5ths on the staff

Melodic 5ths   Harmonic 5ths

5ths on the keyboard skip three white keys.
5ths on the staff move from a space to a space skipping one space,
or a line to a line skipping one line.

Melodic 5ths

12. Draw a melodic 5th **up** from each given note. Use quarter notes. Name each note.

13. Draw a melodic 5th **down** from each given note. Use half notes. Name each note.

Harmonic 5ths

14. Draw a note above each given note to form harmonic 5ths. Use whole notes. Name the notes

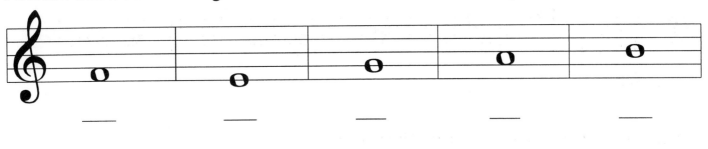

15. Name each interval (2nd, 3rd, 4th or 5th).

Unit 6
Sharps, Flats, and Naturals

Sharp Sign ♯

A **sharp** sign before a note tells you to play the very next key *higher*.

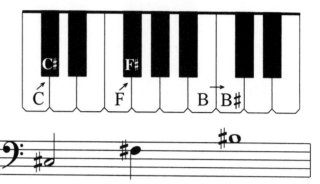

Sharps are written on lines or in spaces.

1. Most sharps are black keys. There are two white key sharps. One is B♯.
   Name the other white key sharp. _____

2. Draw a sharp before each note below. Make sure the center of the sharp is in the same space or on the same line as the note. Name each sharp note.

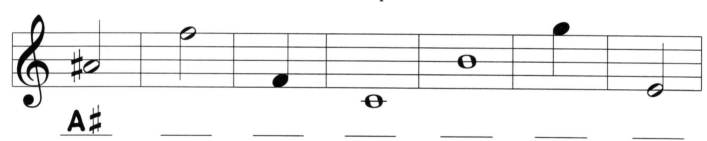

A♯ _____ _____ _____ _____ _____ _____

3. Name these sharp notes. Circle the ones that will be white keys.

A♯ _____ _____ _____ _____ _____ _____ _____

4. Draw these sharp notes on the staff. Use whole notes.

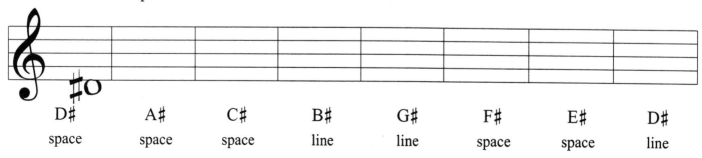

D♯	A♯	C♯	B♯	G♯	F♯	E♯	D♯
space	space	space	line	line	space	space	line

Flat Sign ♭

A **flat** sign before a note tells you to play the very next key *lower*.

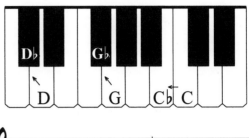

Flats are written on lines or in spaces.

5. Most flats are black keys. There are two white key flats. One is C♭.
   Name the other white key flat._____

6. Draw a flat before each note below. Make sure the center of the flat is in the same space or on the same line as the note. Name each flat note.

G♭

7. Name these flat notes. Circle the ones that will be white keys.

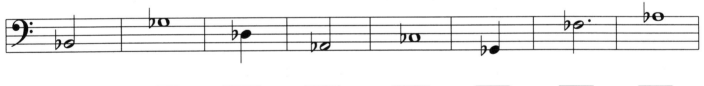

8. Draw these flat notes on the staff. Use quarter notes.

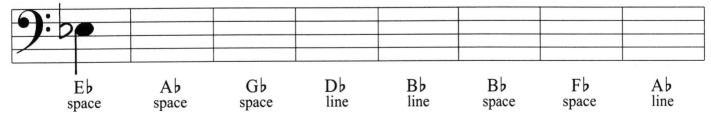

E♭	A♭	G♭	D♭	B♭	B♭	F♭	A♭
space	space	space	line	line	space	space	line

Natural Sign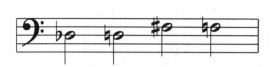

A **natural** sign before a note *cancels* any sharp or flat.

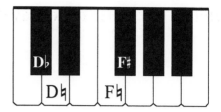

Naturals are written on lines or in spaces   Natural notes are always white keys.

9. Draw a natural before the second note in each measure below. Make sure the center of the natural is in the same space or on the same line as the note. Name each note.

C♯   C♮   __   __   __   __   __   __

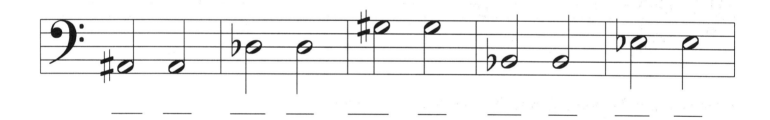

__   __   __   __   __   __   __   __

10. Draw a natural before the second and fourth beat of each measure.
    Play and name the notes.

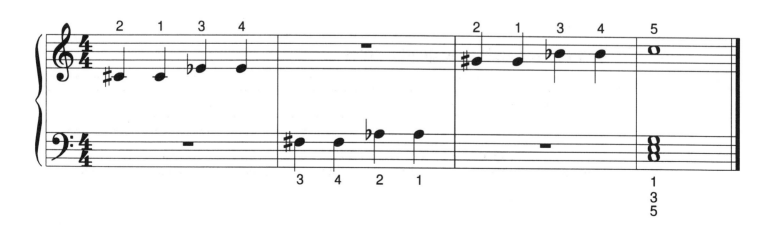

Accidentals

Accidental is the name for any sharp, flat, or natural that appears in music. When an accidental appears in music, it lasts for an entire measure. The bar line at the end of a measure cancels the accidental.

11. Circle the notes to be played **sharp.**

12. Circle the notes to be played **flat.**

Enharmonic Notes

Notes that sound the same but are written differently are called **enharmonic** notes.
Example: F♯ and G♭ are the same key on the piano, but are written differently.

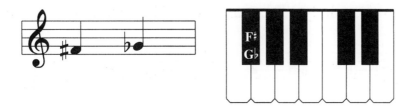

13. Draw the enharmonic note for each given note. Name the notes.

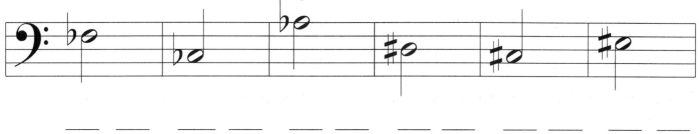

Unit 7
Half Steps and Whole Steps

Half Steps

A **half step** is the distance from one key the very next key with no key between. Half steps can look three different ways on the keyboard:

 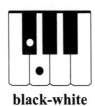 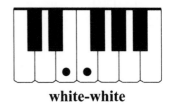

white-black   **black-white**   **white-white**

1. Draw a half step **above** each given note. Use whole notes. Name each note.

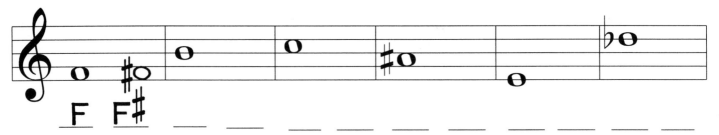

F   F♯   ___   ___   ___   ___

2. Draw a half step **below** each given note. Use half notes. Name each note.

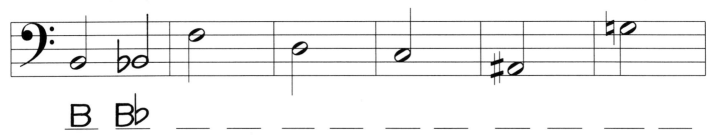

B   B♭   ___   ___   ___   ___

3. Circle the half steps in this melody. There are five. *(The first is done for you.)*

4. Name two half steps that are black-white.   1.___ to ___   2.___ to ___

5. Name two half steps that are white-black.   1.___ to ___   2.___ to ___

6. Name two half steps that are white-white.   1.___ to ___   2.___ to ___

7. Are there any half steps that are black-black? Circle your answer.   YES   NO

Whole Steps

A **whole step** is the distance from one key to the next key with one key between. Whole steps can look four different ways on the keyboard:

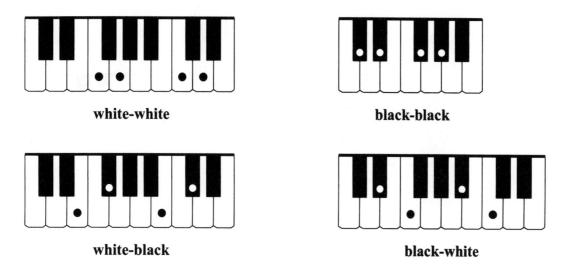

white-white   black-black

white-black   black-white

8. Draw a whole step **above** each given note. Use whole notes. Name each note.

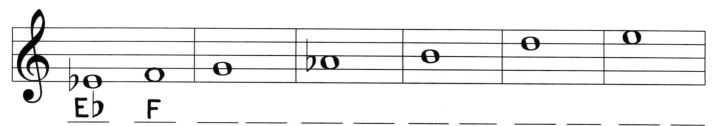

Eb   F

9. Draw a whole step **below** each given note. Use quarter notes. Name each note.

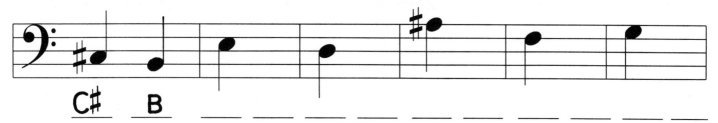

C#   B

10. Circle the whole steps in this melody. There are four.

11. Name two whole steps that are white-white.   1.___ to ___   2.___ to ___

12. Name two whole steps that are black-black.   1.___ to ___   2 ___ to ___

13. Name two whole steps that are white-black.   1.___ to ___   2.___ to ___

14. Name two whole steps that are black-white.   1.___ to ___   2.___ to ___

Unit 8
5-Finger Patterns and Triads

Major 5-Finger Patterns

Major 5-finger patterns have five notes formed in a pattern of whole steps and half steps. The half step is between the 3rd and 4th notes of the 5-finger pattern.

C Major 5-Finger Pattern

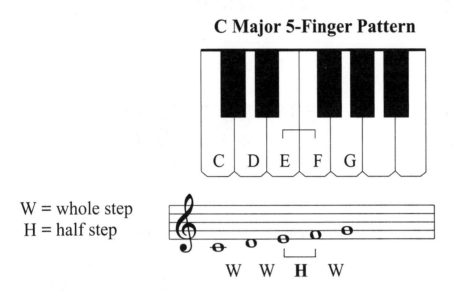

W = whole step
H = half step

W W **H** W

A 5-finger pattern may begin on any note. The lowest note names the 5-finger pattern.

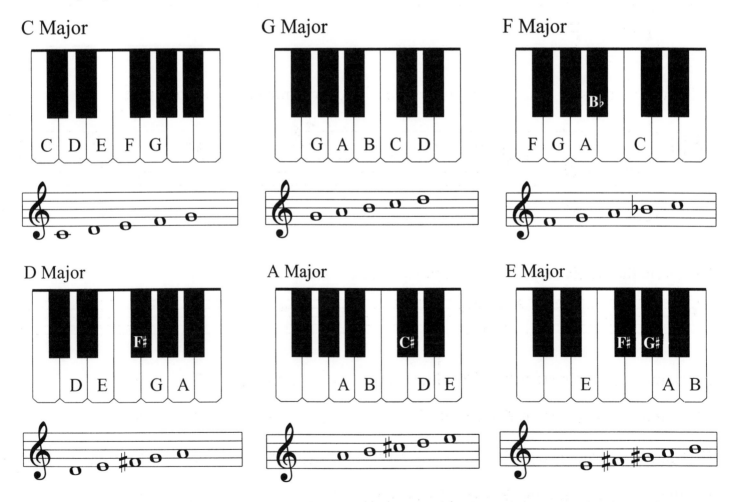

C Major

G Major

F Major

D Major

A Major

E Major

1. Write letters on the keyboards to form Major 5-finger patterns.
2. Draw the notes on the staff. Use whole notes.

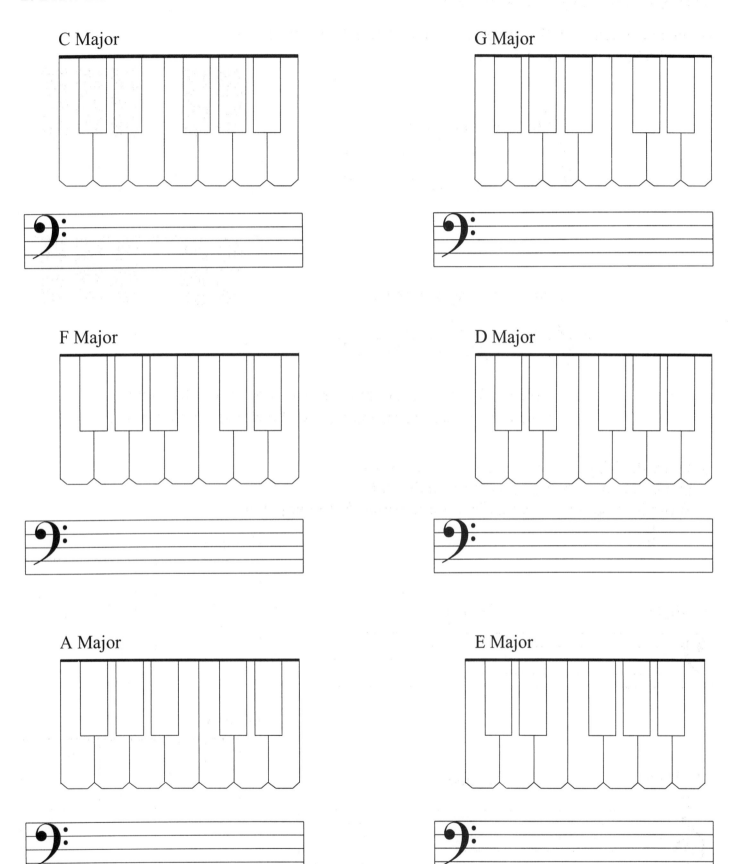

C Major

G Major

F Major

D Major

A Major

E Major

Minor 5-Finger Patterns

To change a **Major** 5-finger pattern into a **minor** 5-finger pattern,
lower the third note one half step.

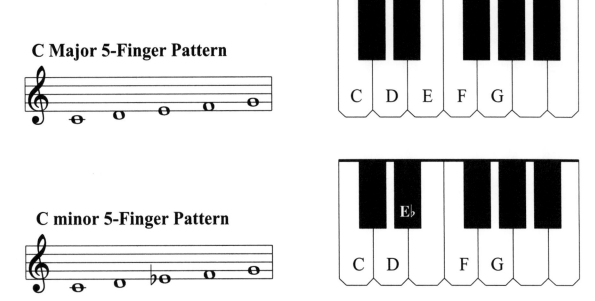

C Major 5-Finger Pattern

C minor 5-Finger Pattern

If the third note is a natural note, it will become a flat note.
If the third note is a sharp note, it will become a natural note.

3. Draw the Major 5-finger patterns on the staff.
   Draw the minor 5-finger patterns on the staff.
   Write letters on the keyboards to form **minor** 5- finger patterns.

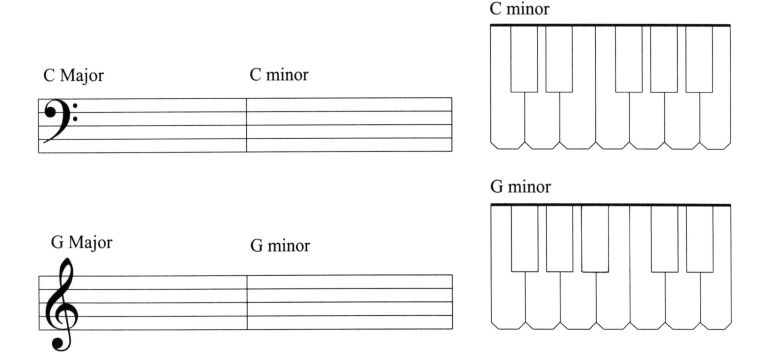

C Major   C minor

G Major   G minor

C minor

G minor

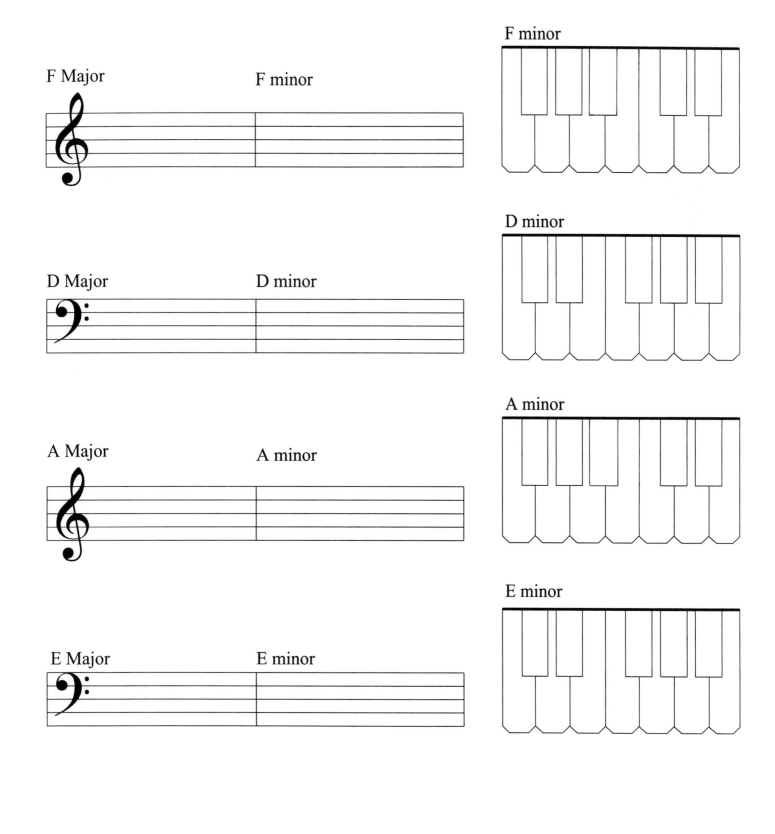

F Major   F minor

F minor

D Major   D minor

D minor

A Major   A minor

A minor

E Major   E minor

E minor

4. Name these 5-finger patterns.

C Major _____   _____   _____   _____

Major Triads

A **triad** is a three note chord.
The 1st, 3rd, and 5th notes of a Major 5-finger pattern form a Major triad.
The notes in a triad are called the **Root**, the **3rd**, and the **5th**.

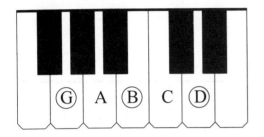

5th ___D___
3rd ___B___
Root ___G___

5. Study the example above and then follow these steps for completing the Major 5-finger patterns and triads on the keyboards and staffs below.

   a. Write the letters on the keyboards to form Major 5-finger patterns. Circle the root, the 3rd, and the 5th in each Major 5-finger pattern.

   b. Draw the Major 5-finger patterns on the staff. Use whole notes. Color in the 1st, 3rd, and 5th notes with your pencil.

   c. Draw the Major triad on the staff. Name the root, 3rd, and 5th.

C Major 5-Finger Pattern and Triad

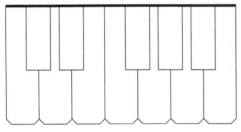

5th _____
3rd _____
Root _____

G Major 5-Finger Pattern and Triad

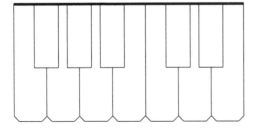

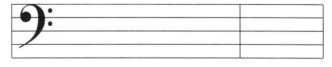

5th _____
3rd _____
Root _____

F Major 5-Finger Pattern and Triad

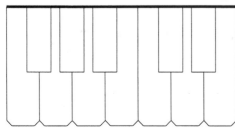

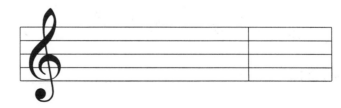

5th _____
3rd _____
Root _____

D Major 5-Finger Pattern and Triad

A Major 5-Finger Pattern and Triad

E Major 5-Finger Pattern and Triad

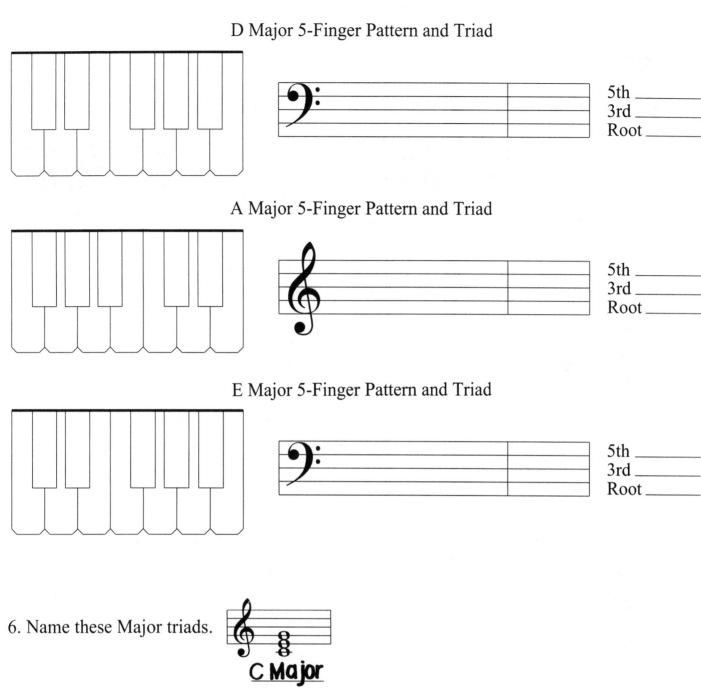

6. Name these Major triads.

C Major

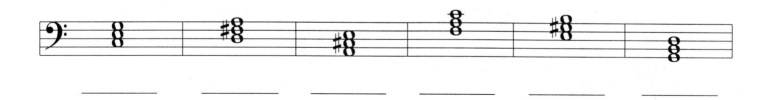

Minor Triads

To change a Major triad into a **minor** triad, lower the 3rd one half step.

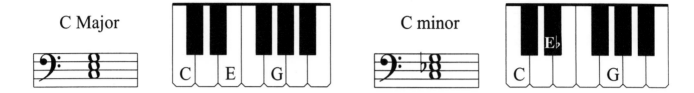

If the 3rd is a natural note, it will become a flat note.
If the 3rd is a sharp note, it will become a natural note.

Reminder: The bar line cancels any accidental in the measure before.
It is not necessary to draw the natural sign.

7. Draw these Major and minor triads

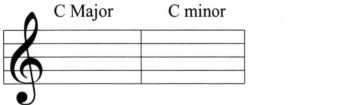

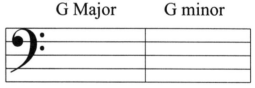

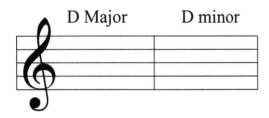

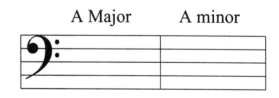

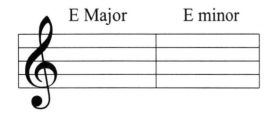

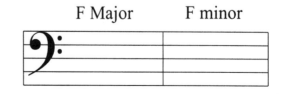

8. Name these minor triads.

_____   _____   _____   _____   _____   _____

_____   _____   _____   _____   _____   _____

Triad Review

9. Draw these Major triads.

C Major   G Major   F Major   D Major   A Major   E Major

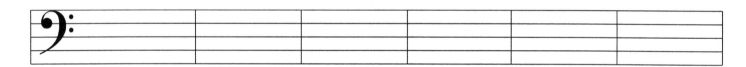

C Major   G Major   F Major   D Major   A Major   E Major

10. Draw these minor triads.

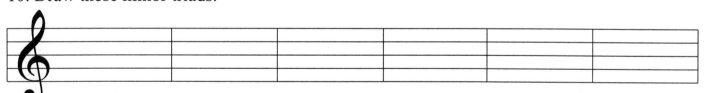

C minor   G minor   F minor   D minor   A minor   E minor

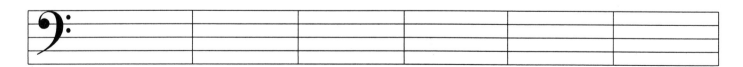

C minor   G minor   F minor   D minor   A minor   E minor

Unit 9

Tetrachords and Major Scales

A **tetrachord** is a group of four notes formed in a pattern of whole steps and half steps.*
The pattern for a Major tetrachord is **whole step - whole step - half step** (W - W - H).

C Major Tetrachord

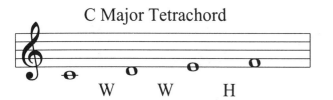

G Major Tetrachord

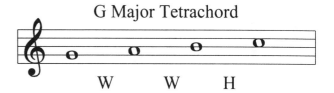

Major scales can be formed by joining two tetrachords.
- The 1st tetrachord is called the **tonic tetrachord.**
- The 2nd tetrachord is called the **dominant tetrachord.**
- The two tetrachords are joined by a whole step.

C Major Scale

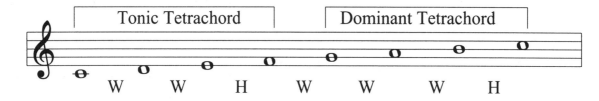

Drawing Major Tetrachords and Scales

1. Draw each Major tetrachord. Then, draw the Major scale by joining the tetrachords.
   (The first note of each tetrachord and scale is drawn for you.)

C Major Tetrachord

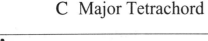

G Major Tetrachord

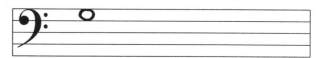

C Major Scale

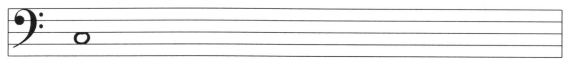

* The first four notes of a Major 5-finger pattern form a Major tetrachord.

G Major Tetrachord

D Major Tetrachord

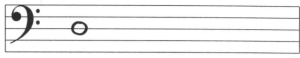

G Major Scale

F Major Tetrachord

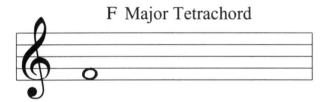

C Major Tetrachord

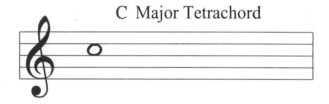

F Major Scale

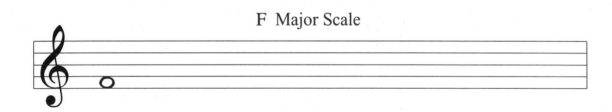

2. Add the correct sharp to make this a G Major scale. Circle the half steps.

3. Add the correct flat to make this an F Major scale. Circle the half steps.

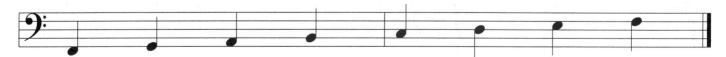

Unit 10
Key Signatures

The **key signature** is the sharps or flats at the beginning of each staff. It tells you:
- notes to be sharp or flat in a piece, and
- the tonic note, or **key,** of the piece.

Major Key Signatures

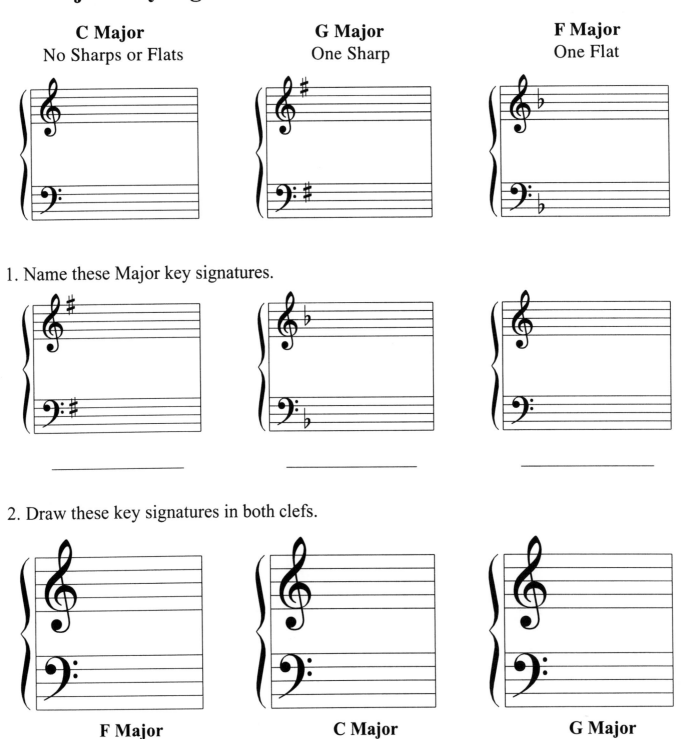

C Major
No Sharps or Flats

G Major
One Sharp

F Major
One Flat

1. Name these Major key signatures.

2. Draw these key signatures in both clefs.

F Major   **C Major**   **G Major**

3. Name the key signature for each example. Circle notes to be played sharp or flat.
   Play each example.

Key of _____

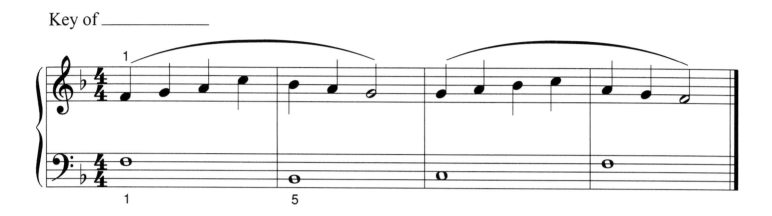

Key of _____

Key of _____

Minor Key Signatures

Each Major key signature has a **relative minor** key signature with the same sharps or flats.

A minor
No sharps or flats
(Relative to C Major)

E minor
One sharp
(Relative to G Major)

D minor
One flat
(Relative to F Major)

4. Name these minor key signatures.

_____

_____

_____

5. Draw these key signatures in both clefs.

D minor

A minor

E minor

6. Three of these melodies are in Major keys and three are in minor keys.
   Determine which ones are Major and which are minor. Name each key signature.

Key of _____

Key of _____

Key of _____

Key of _____

Key of _____

Key of _____

Unit 11
Signs and Terms

Dynamics

Dynamic signs tell how loud or soft to play.

TERM	SIGN	MEANING
piano	*p*	soft
forte	*f*	loud
mezzo piano	*mp*	medium soft
mezzo forte	*mf*	medium loud
crescendo (cresc.)	———◁	gradually louder
diminuendo (dim.)	◁———	gradually softer

1. Write the term and sign after the meaning.

MEANING	SIGN	TERM
soft	_____	_____
loud	_____	_____
medium soft	_____	_____
medium loud	_____	_____
gradually louder	_____	_____
gradually softer	_____	_____

Tempo

Tempo marks tell how fast or slow to play.

TERM	MEANING
allegro	fast (also means cheerful, happy)
allegretto	somewhat fast (slower than allegro)
andante	walking tempo (flowing)
andantino	slightly faster than andante
con moto	with motion
lento	slow
moderato	moderately

Changing Tempo

a tempo	return to the original tempo
ritardando (rit.)	gradually slower

2. Write the term after the meaning.

MEANING	TERM
fast (also means cheerful, happy)	_____
somewhat fast (slower than allegro)	_____
walking tempo (flowing)	_____
slightly faster than andante	_____
with motion	_____
slow	_____
moderately	_____
return to the original tempo	_____
gradually slower	_____

Articulation

Articulation signs tell how to touch and release keys.

TERM	SIGN	MEANING
accent		strong emphasis
legato		smooth, connected
staccato		short, detached
tenuto		hold full value; slight emphasis

3. Write the term and sign after the meaning

MEANING	TERM	SIGN
short, detached	_____	_____
smooth, connected	_____	_____
strong emphasis	_____	_____
hold full value; slight emphasis	_____	_____

Character or Style

These words help establish feeling, mood, or performance style.

TERM	MEANING
cantabile	in a singing manner
dolce	gently, sweetly

4. Write the term after the meaning

MEANING	TERM
in a singing manner	_____
gently, sweetly	_____

More Signs and Terms

D. C. al Fine

D. C. is the abbreviation for **Da capo,** which means *from the head.*
In music, D. C. means to play again from the beginning. **Fine** means *end.*

Play both lines of music, then go back to the beginning and play to the *fine*,
without the repeat.

Fermata 𝄐

A **fermata** sign means to hold a note longer than its time value.

Slur

A **slur** is a curved line over or under two or more notes that are to be played *legato*.
Legato means to play smooth, connected.

Tie

A **tie** is a curved line that connects notes on the same line or space.
Play only the first note and hold it for the value of both notes.

52

Matching and Crossword Puzzle

1. Draw a line to match each item with the correct answer.

Across

6.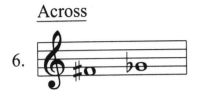

8. fast (also: happy, cheerful)

9.

11. The distance between two notes.

12.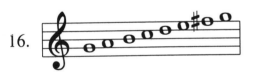

14. soft

15. somewhat fast

16.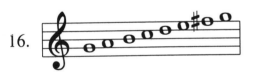

19. Major 5-finger Pattern

21. ♭

22. short, detached

Answers

legato

Major triad

tie

enharmonic notes

natural sign

half step

andante

allegro

key signatures

interval

forte

ABCDE

piano

CDEFG

F Major scale

diminuendo

flat sign

staccato

allegretto

mp

G Major scale

sharp sign

Down

1.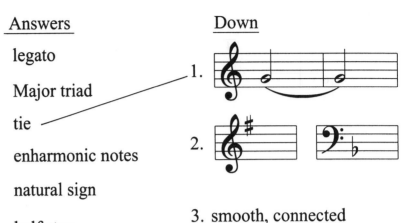

2.

3. smooth, connected

4. ♮

5. walking speed (flowing)

7. medium soft

10. gradually softer

13. loud

17. minor 5-finger pattern

18. ♯

20.

GP660

2. Write the answers in this crossword puzzle.

Unit 12
Transposing

To **transpose** music, play the same pattern of intervals beginning on a different note.

This melody uses the notes of the C Major 5-finger pattern.

Here is the same melody **transposed** to the G Major 5-finger pattern.

1. Begin on F and transpose the melody to the F Major 5-finger pattern.

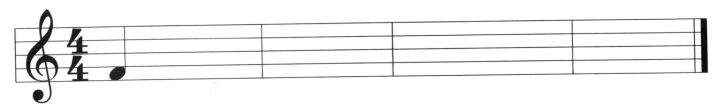

This melody uses the notes of the G Major 5-finger pattern.

2. Begin on D and transpose the melody to the D Major 5-finger pattern.

This piece uses the notes of the A minor 5-finger pattern.

3. Transpose to the C minor 5-finger pattern.

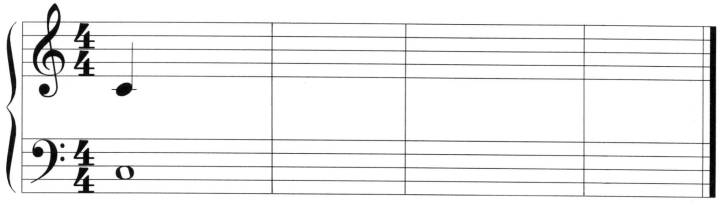

This piece uses the notes of the G Major 5-finger pattern.

4. Transpose to the F Major 5-finger pattern.

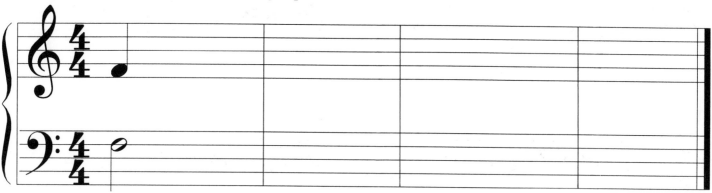

Unit 13
Ear Training

Listen as your teacher plays one interval from each pair. Circle the one you hear.

1.

2.
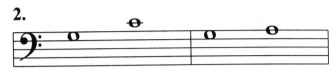

3.
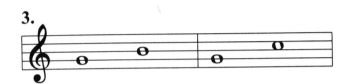

4.

5.

6.

Listen as your teacher plays a Major or minor 5-finger pattern. Circle the one you hear.

7.

8.

9.

10.

11.
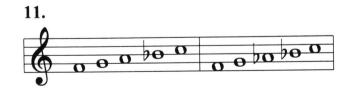

12.
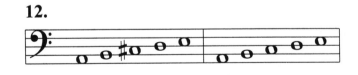

Listen as your teacher plays a Major or minor triad. Circle the one you hear.

13.

14.

15.
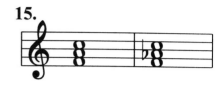

16.
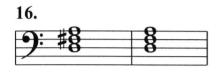

17.
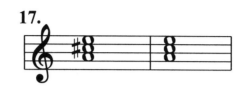

18.

Listen as your teacher plays one melody from each pair. Circle the one you hear.

19.

20.

Listen as your teacher taps one rhythm from each pair. Circle the one you hear.

21.
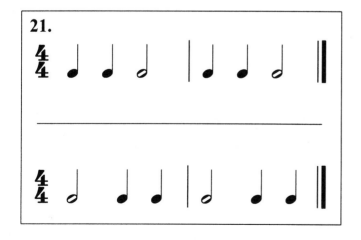

22.
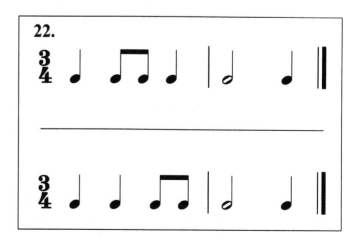

Unit 14
Sight Reading

The best way to become a good sight reader is to read new music every day.

1. Before you sight read, look through the entire piece and observe:
    - key signature
    - time signature
    - clef signs
    - dynamics
    - accidentals
    - slurs, ties, staccatos, accents, etc.
    - rhythmic and melodic patterns

2. Find the first note and finger number for each hand.

3. Play slowly.
    - Use a metronome to keep a steady beat.
    - Count one measure aloud before you begin to play.
    - Continue to count aloud as you play.

4. Keep your eyes on the music.
    - Avoid looking up and down from the music to your hands.
    - Look ahead to see what is next.

5. Keep going, even if you make some mistakes: avoid going back to fix anything.

Allegro

After you sight read:

1. Evaluate your playing
    - Were the notes and rhythm correct?
    - Were the dynamics and articulation markings clear and distinct?
    - Did the music continue to move forward as you maintained a steady beat?

2. Sight read the music again.
    - Concentrate on correcting any previous mistakes.
    - Set a goal for a perfect performance by the third reading.

Andantino

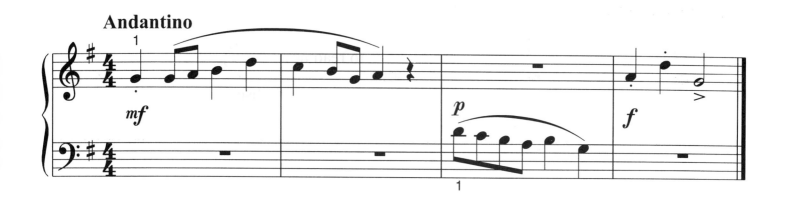

Allegretto

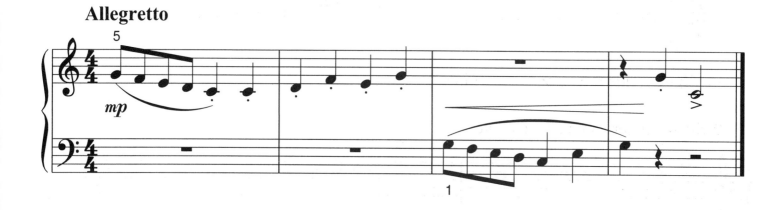

Cantabile

Con moto

Review Test

1. Name these notes.

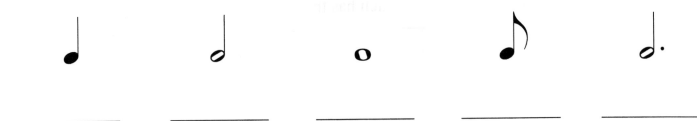

_____ _____ _____ _____ _____

2. This is a _____ . 3. This is a _____ .

4. Bar lines divide music on the staff into _____ .

5. Write the letter name of each note.

_____ _____ _____ _____ _____ _____ _____

6. This is a _____ .

2 means _____ .

4 means _____ .

7. Write the counts under these notes.

8. Draw a note in the box below the rest which has the same value.

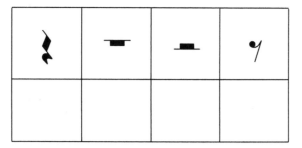

9. Write in the counts.

10. Name these melodic intervals.

_____ _____ _____ _____

11. Name these harmonic intervals.

_____ _____ _____ _____

12. Name these signs.

 #   b   ♮

_____ _____ _____

13. Draw these notes. Use whole notes.

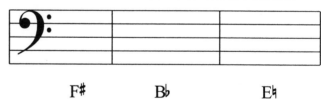

F#   B♭   E♮

14. Draw the enharmonic note for each given note. Name each note.

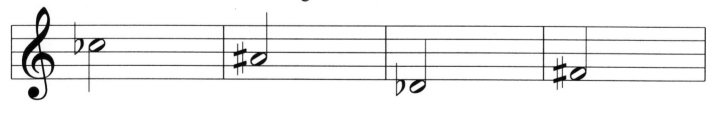

_____ _____ _____ _____

15. Write **W** for whole step and **H** for half step.

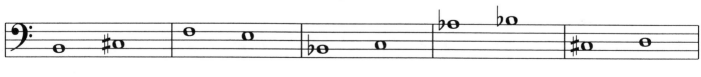

_____ _____ _____ _____

16. Name these 5-finger patterns.

_____   _____   _____   _____

17. Draw these 5-finger patterns.

G Major   E minor

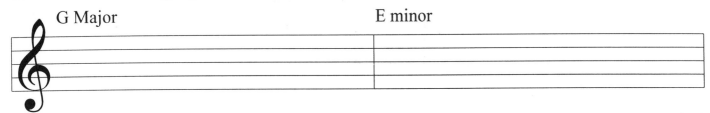

A Major   G minor

18. Name these triads.

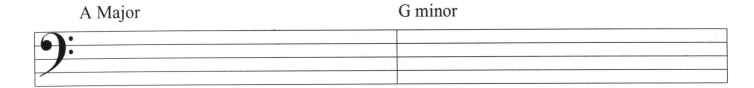

_____   _____   _____   _____   _____   _____

19. Draw these triads.

F minor   D Major   E minor   G Major   A minor   C minor

20. Add the correct sharp or flat to form these Major scales.

G Major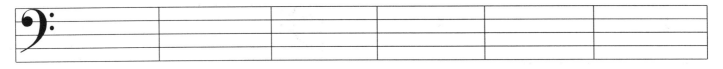

F Major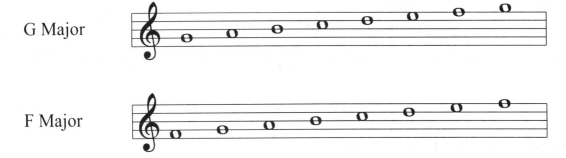

21. Name these key signatures.

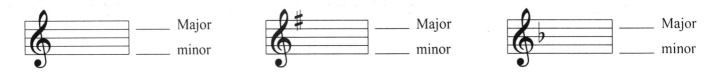

_____ Major   _____ Major   _____ Major

_____ minor   _____ minor   _____ minor

22. Draw lines to match the terms with the signs.

accent

tie

repeat

fermata

slur

tenuto

23. Write the term for each meaning.

_____ loud

_____ smooth, connected

_____ gently, sweetly

_____ walking speed

_____ gradually slower

_____ moderately

_____ medium soft

_____ somewhat fast

24. Write the terms for these signs.

_____   _____   _____

25. What does *D. C. al Fine* mean?

_____

26. Write the meaning for each term.

crescendo _____   diminuendo _____

cantabile _____   allegro _____

27. Study this music and answer the questions below.

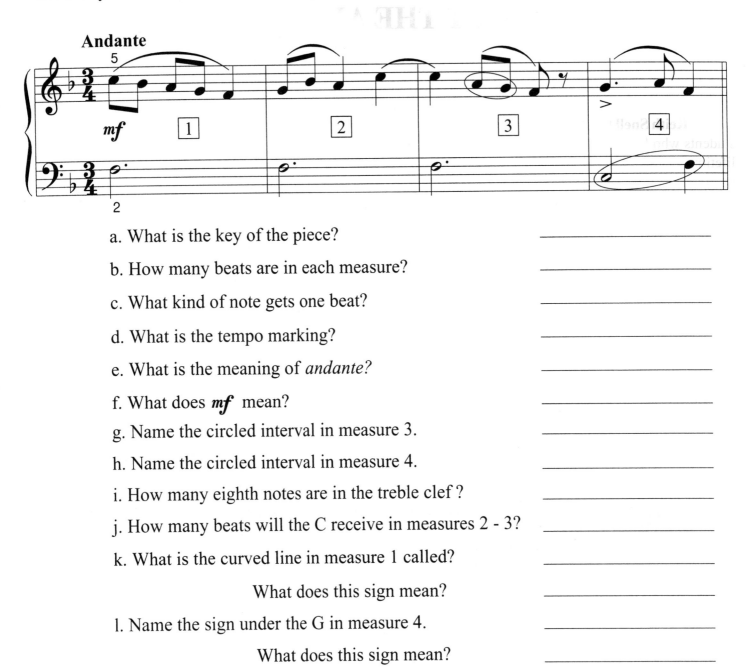

a. What is the key of the piece? _____

b. How many beats are in each measure? _____

c. What kind of note gets one beat? _____

d. What is the tempo marking? _____

e. What is the meaning of *andante?* _____

f. What does *mf* mean? _____

g. Name the circled interval in measure 3. _____

h. Name the circled interval in measure 4. _____

i. How many eighth notes are in the treble clef ? _____

j. How many beats will the C receive in measures 2 - 3? _____

k. What is the curved line in measure 1 called? _____

        What does this sign mean? _____

l. Name the sign under the G in measure 4. _____

        What does this sign mean? _____

28. Transpose this melody to the D Major 5-finger pattern.